D0385142

To: _____

WHAT I LOVE
ABOUT US

I love our

_____ .

I love how good we are at

_____.

3

We'd make the best

_____

team ever.

I love to watch

_____

with you.

5

I love how much you make me

_____

when you

_____ .

Playing

with you is my favorite.

When we're apart, it makes me happy
to think about our

_____ .

If you and I were wild animals, we'd be

_____ .

9

I wish we'd known each other when

_____ .

I love how we make each other feel so

_____ .

I love how we always go

_____ .

12

I love the

_____

ritual we have.

13

We always have the greatest time

_____ .

14

I love how we

_____

every day.

15

I love sharing

_____

with you.

16

Being with you makes me want to be a better

_____ .

17

Let's make a

_____

again soon.

18

We should totally

_____

together.

19

We deserve the

_____

award.

20

I love dreaming about

_____

with you.

21

If we were a city, we'd be

_____ .

22

It's so funny when we

_____ .

23

I love how good we are at giving each other

_____ .

24

I still can't believe we

_____ .

25

The story of how we

_____

is so awesome.

26

If we wanted to, we could easily

_____ .

27

I love how you

_____

my

_____ .

28

I wish we were flying to

_____

tonight.

29

It is incredibly sweet when we

_____ .

30

I love that we share the same taste in

_____ .

31

We make the best

_____ .

32

I love remembering the time we

_____

and

_____ .

33

I believe the world needs our unique

———————————————————————————— .

34

I am so glad we

_____ .

35

Everyone should be as

_____

as we are.

36

I love it when we

_____

like

_____ .

37

I love how we never get tired of

_____ .

38

I love

_____

with you on the weekends.

39

We need to

---

again.

40

I love creating

_____

together.

If we could just

_____

we'd be

_____ .

42

If we were a song, we'd be

_____ .

I am a little bit obsessed with our

_____ .

44

I love how we

_____

each other.

45

You are my favorite

_____

in the world.

Nobody else can

---

like us.

47

I am so

_____

that we're

_____ .

It'd be great if we could

_____

together one day.

49

I'd love it if we were

_____

right now.

I hope our

_____

lasts forever.

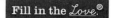

Created, published and, distributed by Knock Knock
1635-B Electric Ave.
Venice, CA 90291
knockknockstuff.com
Knock Knock is a registered trademark of Knock Knock LLC
Fill in the Love is a registered trademark of Knock Knock LLC

© 2015 Knock Knock LLC
All rights reserved
Made in China

ISBN: 978-160106758-6   **UPC:** 825703-50074-5